# Management C.R.A.P.  I Learned, That Seems to Work

## Second Edition

BY

### James R. Guenther
### The Recovering Accountant

Management C.R.A.P. I Learned, That
Seems To Work. Second Edition

Copyright © 2015 by James R. Guenther

Edited by Kathleen Gardner and Kari Bendall

Cover by Al Haas, Brandxlerator

ISBN 978-1-329-58725-0

First published in the United States by Lulu

This book is dedicated to the most important people in my life: my family and my extended family. Special thanks to my son Jeremy who encouraged me to finally do this.

# Table of Contents

# Introduction.

Over the years, I can't believe how much I have learned about people and people in business. I certainly do believe I am better at managing people and situations today than I was when I got out of school. I guess that experience is an excellent teacher. I do find it surprising however how many managers don't learn from their experiences and therefore keep making the same mistakes over and over. I guess people get set in their ways and don't change their basic positions or beliefs. My own personal mission in life has been to "serve the Lord, help people, and make a little difference". That's what I'm trying to do here. My gift was the ability to take systems and people and get them to work together very effectively, which improved efficiency and overall company quality. I've always said that I'm not the smartest guy in the world, but I can outwork most people, and that counts in this world. I was always willing to do any job to help my boss and my company. I never cared to be in the spotlight, but I learned at times it can't be helped. Then it's good to use the spotlight to your advantage.

I genuinely like people and I like working with them and for their benefit. I also like to run things and as I have told my wife, I work most effectively with people that do what I say. (I'm kidding about that.) I love to listen to the ideas of others and take advantage of their ideas whenever possible.

I never cared for long winded speeches, so it follows that my thoughts are pretty much concise and short.

I've done four turnarounds from the inside of companies. All of them were difficult. I've been in construction machinery, steel, chemicals, promotional products, non-profit and what I call "management guidance". I have heard many times "our business is different". I know there are subtleties, but I am convinced that most businesses and markets work off of the same principles: a good product or service, a company that takes care of its people, good people working hard, honesty, and above all, taking care of the customer.

I've used the term "recovering accountant". When I finished high school, I wandered through academic majors for a while. My dad, a banker, suggested accounting because he thought it was a really good way to get to know a company from the inside out. So, I majored in accounting, liked it, and got a job with a CPA firm. I moved on to private industry. First I wanted to be a supervisor, then manager. Next I wanted the title of Controller, then VP Finance, and then President. I think I made a transition from a strictly numbers guy to all around business guy - something a lot of accountants aren't able to do. That was my "recovery". My transition was mostly about the challenge, and doing it better than anyone else had done it. I ended up at the top of the organizations. I did it myself. My dad didn't own the company.

I have often asked myself "Why me?" How did the "recovering accountant" end up as the CEO? I have three answers. The Good Lord. Desire to move up the ladder. And willingness to work hard.

I hope what I have to say is thought provoking for you, and perhaps my ideas or some variation of them, will be of help to you. It is the "help people" portion of my personal mission.

# Excellence.

Excellence is one of my favorite words, and in order to achieve it, the subject that must be on our business minds at all times. It is a word we need to use a lot - from the top to the bottom of the business. So I liked to display big banners prominently in the office, warehouse, and manufacturing facility: Excellence in all we do. We have an excellent product sold to excellent customers, by excellent employees. That's the idea—now we need to make it happen. It is my belief that if we tell our employees we expect excellence, we have taken a big step in achieving it. There is more, however. We cannot accept mediocrity. If we have a mediocre employee who performs in a mediocre manner, over time, we need to make a change. Excellence breeds excellence and accepting mediocrity means more of it.

In the businesses where I worked, achieving excellence would have been hard without a total quality (management?) program. Obviously, there are many books written on the subject, many classes to attend, and a lot of consultants who make a lot of money talking about TQM. My definition of TQM (Total Quality Management) was pretty simple on the surface. Measure everything, from product development, orders taken, manufacturing, service, shipping, to collection of the receivable. It is not easy to find measurements for everything. It takes thinking creatively and some trial and error. It is hard to find improvement without a comparison and baselines, and that's why TQM is so critical. I also found that if I started measuring things, I got better at it, and discovered new measurements that I hadn't thought of before. I found that the work in setting up a quality system was well worth the investment in time and money.

I would tell employees when coming out of a turnaround that we want to be an excellent company with excellent products delivered in an excellent manner by excellent employees who have excellent pay and benefits. I really believed that and worked toward it every day. I posted the large banners in all work areas so employees saw the word all the while they worked. We, as managers, need to help our employees achieve excellence, perhaps by explaining how to make a better product, make it faster, and, therefore, at a lower cost.

Why excellence? It is a very effective way to survive and thrive in today's business climate. You have to be the best or begin that journey, and get there as soon as you can. Excellent products are easier to sell, have less warranty cost, and employees are proud to be associated with these excellent products.

Mediocrity is a word I don't like, but we are often too willing to accept it in the hiring of employees, their performance, their skills, in product development, in sales, and in all we do, including the way we live our lives.

Unions did many good things in our developing nation. Now I believe they have basically been replaced by the government, except in one area for sure. Unions protect mediocrity. I am reminded of a union steward I knew who quit as the steward because he was tired of defending employees who deserved to lose their jobs due to continued tardiness or absence.

Employees whose work and work ethic are poor are the employees that I, as a manager, want to be gone as soon as possible. They don't belong in my excellent workplace.

I suggest you use the word excellence often in front of your employees, so they know that excellence is important to you. Then, more often than not, it will be important to them.

## Thinking is Hard Work. That's Why We Don't See More of It.

Sometimes I would sit in meetings on a given subject and absolutely marvel at some of the answers people would give to various questions. It became clear that they had given little thought to the subject before they walked through the meeting room door. It wasn't unusual for someone to later say "I guess that doesn't make much sense now that I think about it". So often, I thought I was the only one in the room that had done any thinking about a serious subject. At the same time, however, I literally scheduled specific time for thinking. I believe most people don't do that. They're too busy making sales, taking phone calls, filling orders, and attending to their daily routines etc., to really give serious thought to a subject. I also thought that as CEO, it was my duty to think about the whole operation—really think and reason.

One of my favorite business subjects was always strategic planning. I especially enjoyed teaching it, because it essentially had no application boundaries. Nearly any business issue was fair game for discussion. That made the class fun and interesting. When I did some consulting on strategic planning with business owners, it also became clear to me that many business owners thought very little about their future or the future of their business. Why? They thought about engineering, sales, operations, orders in and orders out, but seldom thought about the future, unless there was some significant event that caused them to think about it, like the death of a partner, health issues, turnaround of the business, or something similar. And like the cat said to Alice in Wonderland at the fork in the road, "if you don't know where you are going, it doesn't matter how you get there".

My suggestion is set aside time for thinking—and planning.

**Some of the Employee Traits We Criticize are the Same Traits that Make the Employee Good at Their Jobs Under Different Circumstances.**

Did you ever have an employee who just wouldn't let go of something? Sure, we all have. Whatever it is, they think it should be changed, and right now! We think the idea has merit but we just haven't gotten around to it. At the infamous annual review, we bring up that employee's persistence. It's a bad thing, right? Well, what if that employee is a superb credit and collections person? That persistence is one of the best attributes for that job—and we just criticized the employee for it.

Or, what about the employee who is rather outspoken, to the point that, as a supervisor, we can't believe they even brought up a given situation. But, perhaps that trait is just what is needed to open new accounts. They are willing to ask anyone almost anything and that fearless approach has paid off. It's better than burying their head in the sand, right?

What is my point? We should be aware of employee personality traits, and choose our criticisms carefully. Maybe it is necessary for an employee to tone down their customer approach, but we, as supervisors, must understand what, exactly, makes an employee effective at their job.

# Wander Around.

A number of years ago there was an author who suggested "Management by Wandering Around". So, this thought isn't a new one, but I certainly stumbled upon it by myself as opposed to reading it in a book. Don't get me wrong, I love books but I tend to be a rather social person and I discovered that if I talked to people outside of my office or on the shop floor, they would share what turned out to invaluable information. Certainly, I was aware that there may be an agenda behind the information the employees shared, but that was alright. If I could right a wrong and make the company a better place, so be it.

At one company where I worked, we measured our direct production costs on a per ton of product basis. It was amazing how steady the comparisons from month to month could be. And if there was a variance, there was usually a pretty good explanation as to why. One month, we had a pretty significant increase in the usage of water. Water was used in a quench tank to cool heated castings. There were water re-circulators that carried water to cooler air on the roof of the plant. What I discovered is that when things got busy, it took too long for the water to be cooled down by the re-circulating pumps, so what the production people did was to turn on the city water to the tank, which caused the tank to overflow into a sewer, but the cold city water cooled down the quench tank much more quickly. Production managers weren't aware of what was being done. A production employee gladly told me the story, thinking he was doing a good thing by cooling more castings more quickly (and raising his hourly pay rate, because he was paid an incentive on a per casting basis). I soon figured out that I could become proactive in reducing costs before they appeared in the financials at the end of the month. I was amazed at what people would tell me. I made the same round almost every morning. I became aware of employee concerns about their work, the company, and even their families.

Another insight I discovered, was that I had to be careful about the way I looked when I wandered around. No long somber faces. If I looked distressed, employees got worried that something was wrong, and that probably wasn't good. So, it was necessary to put on a happy face. I did my deep thinking at home.

So, wander around, be visible, everyday you are in the office.

# Understand the Financials.

There are many courses of study at our colleges and universities. Some of them include courses in accounting or perhaps its entitled, Finance and Accounting, for Non-Financial Managers. To me, these courses are very encouraging because they are evidence of the importance of understanding the financial side of business. I don't see how you can be a responsible business operator without understanding the meanings of the balance sheet and earnings (hopefully) statement of the business. In my experience, many managers have some understanding of the earnings statement, but have no idea what a balance sheet is about.

A balance sheet is a statement of assets, liabilities, and equity as of a specific date, usually the end of a month, or quarter, or year. In business, on the asset side, it would be the amount of cash we have, the accounts receivable we are owed, how much inventory we have and the value of our fixed assets (plant and equipment). Liabilities would be amounts owed to vendors, amounts owed to employees, amounts owed to the government for fees and taxes, to name just a few examples. Equity is the ownership of the company and the accumulated earnings over the life of the business. These are very simplistic examples of the business balance sheet as of a specific point in time. Our personal balance sheet would be how much cash we have as of a specific date, the historical value of our home, cars and other assets. Personal liabilities would perhaps be our unpaid gas bill or electric bill and the amount we owe on our mortgage or cars. Our personal equity would be the amount of ownership we have in our assets. For instance, if we paid $250,000 for our home and currently owe $100,000, our equity is $150,000.

The earnings statement for our business is the revenue earned over a period of time (a month, quarter, or year) less the expenses for the exact same period of time. The result is the amount of money we earned or lost. On the personal side, it would be the amount of income we had from all of our sources, for a period of time, less our personal expenses for the same period. Examples of personal expenses would be our payment of utilities, interest expenses, tuition, food, and the like. Hopefully on the personal side, our earnings exceed our expenses, which mean we might be able to put some money away for savings, or perhaps retirement.

I actually conducted courses for my top managers on the meaning of each line of the balance sheet and earnings statement. Many managers are responsible for a departmental budget and find it interesting to see how their departmental expenses fit into the overall earnings statement.

The closer we get to the top in business, the more we may have to explain our financials to our banker, outside accountant, board members, investors, or potential investors. That calls for a thorough understanding of the financials. Comparative statements are especially useful. How are we doing compared to our plan, or prior year? The answer often leads to why we are doing better or worse, which leads to specific problem areas, which need to be addressed. Outsiders have expectations that the officers of the company understand the balance sheet and earnings statements of their business. Simply having the financial person explain the statements may not be good enough.

## I Believe That the Most Honest Employee Could Steal from You, if You Allow It.

This is another lesson I learned the hard way. One company I worked for allowed employees to cash personal checks with our cashier. The primary duties of the cashier involved providing cash travel advances for employees who were going out of town on company business. This was before the use of credit cards was so prevalent, and there were employees who couldn't get a credit card or didn't believe in them. Employees also felt if they were on company business, it was up to the company to provide them with whatever they needed to travel. The cash box was in the possession of the cashier and carried a pretty good balance, about $5,000. We reconciled the cash box on a monthly basis and never had any trouble. But then, one day, the cash box was short about $20. When that had happened before, the cash usually came out "over" the next time. It didn't work out that way in this case. The shortages continued, which caused the cash box to be counted more frequently, weekly, but small shortages continued. Suspicion began to focus on the cashier, which ultimately led to termination. There was no way that we could prove the cashier was responsible, until after the individual left and we found a variety of IOU's. The cashier had gotten into some financial trouble and started dipping into the cash box. To this day, I think the cashier was a good and basically honest person, as demonstrated by the IOU's. There was intent to repay the money when things got better, but of course, they never did. The cashier was probably too embarrassed and afraid to come to her manager with her financial issue. That's too bad.

I am a recovering accountant by education and I believe we need to do two very important things. Number one, we must set up effective internal controls to do as much as we can to stop employee dishonesty. Secondly, we need to inform employees that if they get themselves into trouble, we are available to help. I recall a single mom who came to me a couple of days before payday and told me she didn't have enough money to feed her two kids that night. There was also a teacher, again a single mom, who could not make her rent because her support check from her ex-husband was delayed, and her manager refused to give her an advance because it wasn't "his problem". Then there was an employee whose wife was involved in an auto accident, where she seriously injured a child. She was extremely distraught and was arrested by police and sat in jail because our employee could not post a $200 bond. I firmly believe helping these employees when they were in great distress, builds long lasting, loyal relationships.

I am also very aware that an employee could take unfair advantage, but I also know it would only happen once.

You can do a lot of good by helping a good employee who is in dire need. Don't be afraid to do so. Know and understand internal controls in your area of responsibility, and ensure they are maintained.

## Employees Most Often Quit Their Bosses, Not the Company.

I am an accountant by education, not the easiest course of study in school, and not the hardest. I remember the first partner I worked for in a CPA firm told me that public accounting was 50% accounting and 50% people skills. Very true and even more true in an industrial setting. The accounting side was a piece of cake compared to the managing of people. I always believed I was a good supervisor, and that was supported by comments I received from employees when they, or I, was leaving the company.

We need to build relationships with our employees and co-workers. There are so many ways to do this. I've been to funerals when an employee has a lost a family member. Attending the funeral takes a small amount of time, but is long-remembered by the employee and family. I mentioned earlier about the employee who came to me and said she didn't have enough money to feed her two kids that night. I reached for my wallet to give her some money, immediately. I mentioned a teacher that didn't have the money to make her rent payment, because her ex-husbands support check didn't arrive. Once again, I reached for my wallet. Those actions are remembered for a long, long time and I believe that those employees are willing to go to greater lengths to accomplish the goals of the department and the company.

It is incredibly important to treat our employees with courtesy, honesty and respect. Keep in mind that I talked about the need for excellent employees and those are the employees I'm talking about. When we have that excellent employee, we have to make every effort to accommodate his or her needs, whether it is for attention, some time off, learning, or understanding. We want the kind of employees who are willing to help out whenever necessary, go the extra mile, and get the job done without being told. When we have that type of employee, we want to keep them. Good pay, good benefits, and a supervisor who appreciates them and lets them know it can mean keeping the good ones. When a manager is Dr. Jekyll or Mr. Hyde and employees don't know who is going to show up, their work life is unsettled. If they are an excellent employee, why put up with that? They are the ones who can usually find another job. Excellent employees, if dissatisfied, are the first to leave, because they can. So, let's do what we can to show that we appreciate their efforts.

I believe that employees can sense when their manager genuinely cares about them as a person. We need to listen to an employee's concerns about their job, the company, and sometimes their personal issues. Often we can steer them towards professional help if it is needed, but often times people just need to "vent".

I am pretty sure that when an employee decides to find another job, it is often related to their immediate superior. Yes, I understand employees leave for a promotion or for more money or their spouse needs to relocate, but there are often many employees who leave because of their poor relationship with their superior. Work everyday to build meaningful relationships with your valued employees.

## Policies are Guidelines, Not Written in Granite and Not "Cover".

If you have been through a strategic planning process, you understand how the vision and mission are supported by strategies, which are supported by goals, objectives, etc., ending with policies which, ultimately, are in support of the vision or mission. Policies are used to provide some consistency in daily operations. Usually, there are lots of them, sometimes written in the employee handbook and sometimes unwritten but often quoted, "it's our policy". Policies are always easy to stand behind, especially when we don't know what else to say, or have little logic to offer. I am often amazed at the managers who can provide no reasoning behind a policy other than, "that's the way it has always been". Policies are not written in granite and CAN be changed. I have sometimes responded to the customer service person at the local department store, "if you can't explain the policy, waive it". That often leads to a conversation with the manager who probably will give us what we want. As they say, "the higher you go, the more you get".

Many companies go through an annual strategic planning process, revising goals and objectives, but seldom review day to day policies that don't make sense under revised strategies. For instance, if we say our employees are our most important resource, why don't our policies support that position?

When it comes to policies, use your head, and don't be afraid to change them or make exceptions to them.

## Employee Personalities are Pretty Much Fixed. Don't Put a Square Peg in a Round Hole.

Many times I have heard the potential bride say, "He's "basically" a good person and I know I can change him". Not likely. I believe the same holds true for employees. Why is it we often take the best sales people and make them sales managers or the best engineers and make them engineering managers when the skill set for the manager position is significantly different than for that of a salesman or engineer? The result sometimes works, but what we have done is moved our employee from a technical position to an administrative/people oriented position. The idea that the best engineer makes the best engineering manager seems flawed to me. Engineering or maybe accounting attracts a certain type of personality. If we take that personality and expect that person to be happy in the managerial field, well, it may not work. Now, let's apply the concept to other positions. The person who works in collections may not make a good customer service person and all the effort we put into training won't change the personality or make a position fulfilling when the person doesn't enjoy what they do.

It is my thought that we can not assume that good performance in one position will necessarily equate to good performance in another position. And I don't believe that, as managers, we pay nearly enough attention to considering employee personality traits when placing employees in their positions.

Obviously, an employee may have "sold" their way into being hired or promoted into a position. That may not be the employee we want on our team, but for an excellent employee, we need to help them find contentment in their positions.

## Perception Versus Reality.

I think being CEO of a medium sized business was one of the loneliest jobs I've ever had. You had to be careful about the look on your face, and whether your door was open or closed. There were things that you couldn't talk about even with your most trusted employee, and your spouse generally didn't understand many of the personalities located around the country. There were people you listened to, and people you tried to listen to, sometimes without much success. I was a great believer in outsiders on the Board, and that was a little different in a family business. The outsiders provided perspective from views outside of our markets and business conditions. That was good, but it wasn't easy to find a really close confidant.

When it came to listening to employees, it was necessary to listen carefully and very objectively. Most of the time employees had their own perspectives that were often influenced by their business biases, relationships, what they heard, and who they listened to. So, what I was hearing was generally their perception of an event. When I hear from my sales manager the reason that someone quit, and perhaps went to work for a competitor, I wonder if that's the sales manager's perception or is it reality. Making the determination took time and often significant follow- up conversations with other concerned parties, but the last thing you wanted to do was make a decision based on poor or false information.

There are a lot of managers out there who make decisions based on the information they receive from a few valued confidants, without ever checking the accuracy of what they heard. That can be dangerous to the business. Be sure you have the  facts before you make critical decisions.

## Sometimes Employees Need a Hug and Sometimes a Kick in the Pants. (Jerry)

The personal problems we experience in our lives, our employees experience also. Many times, we as co-workers, are unaware of the problems of others. I think we need to listen when someone needs to talk. We can offer an opinion if we are asked. We can help, if we are able, with money or a few hours off. But we need to be honest in our opinions and careful with our help. There can be a fine line between helping and enabling.

What about the kick in the pants? That's just about being honest with an employee on their situation. Sometimes we have to simply encourage them to straighten up and do their job—now! Knowing when to "hug" and when to "kick" is the really hard part. It comes with knowing the employees' personalities and history, their needs, and certainly the needs of the business.

I clearly remember a young lady employee who was an excellent employee but had recently developed a real "attitude". I didn't know why. I called her into my office and said that I had noticed a significant change in her demeanor and I questioned whether she might be happier at another company. While she never shared what was bothering her (certainly her prerogative) a few days later she came in and thanked me for the "kick in the pants". She said it was just what she needed to change her attitude.

*We all have the same problems. It's just that the stories are different". (Syl)*

# I Love Incentives.

Incentives are pretty neat in all aspects of life, but especially effective with employees if handled in the correct manner. I have seen incentives work very effectively and I've seen them fail. Failures resulted because the incentive was not well thought out or there wasn't enough money committed to motivate the employees. First, the failure: I am aware of one incentive plan that was constructed to reduce payroll. The business owner decided after careful analysis that it was worth his while to hire an additional employee in one department, rather than having existing employees work overtime. He was able to hire what he thought were a number of good employees, but they would work for a month or two and quit. The owner had not adjusted the incentive plan for an additional employee and, therefore, the existing employees were literally driving the new hires away by being cold and unfriendly (to say the least) towards the new hire.

One of the places that I worked had many payroll incentives. They were based on 50% hourly rate and 50% incentives to equal the total pay for a particular position. So, the base hourly rate was, let's say, $8 per hour, barely a living wage under most circumstances. But an employee could earn another $1 to $15 per hour depending on how productive they were (piecework if you will). That place had some of the hardest working hourly employees I have ever seen.

Another effective use of incentives was in reducing Workers Compensation claims and premiums. The company was spending about $50,000 a month (200 employees) on workers compensation premiums. Yes, this could be dangerous place to work. An incentive plan was created based on weekly, monthly, quarterly, semi-annual and annual lost time accidents. The frequency of measurements was constructed so that if there was an accident in a week, the month, quarter, semiannual periods. The annual goals could still be achieved. There is no point in having an unachievable incentive. Employees see through that very quickly. The business owner set the plan up pledging $80,000 for the year, or about $20,000 per quarter. It worked very well. Lost time accidents dropped dramatically and the incentives were more than covered by a reduction in workers comp premiums. The other interesting aspect was that employees looked out for each other. We had one employee who had stuck his head between a wall and a moving forklift truck not once but three times. The man enjoyed being on Workers Compensation paid time off. Before the incentive, if this guy missed work, it was of no concern to other workers. With the incentive, his accidents affected other employees in the pocketbook, and they watched him.

My final and best incentive story was based on a number of departments that I felt may have been overstaffed. I actually believe most departments are overstaffed. We had an employee that quit and had been making about $12 per hour. I asked the department manager if it was necessary to hire a replacement for the exiting worker. Her reaction was, "of course". I decided to have a meeting with the whole department, about six people. I told them that I wondered if we really needed to replace the person who was leaving. My proposal was that "Donna" earned $12 per hour. If we could eliminate Donna's position, half of her hourly earnings would be a saving for the company, and half would be distributed to the remaining employees as pay increases. They loved the idea. I also asked them not to say anything about this to other departments—that we needed to keep it confidential, in fairness to other employees, knowing full well that the word would get out very quickly.

Sure enough, it wasn't two weeks later that we had someone leave in the UPS department, and I had a visit from the "lead man" telling me he didn't think we needed to replace the employee who was leaving. This incentive plan accomplished two things that I wanted to achieve. First, pay increases for a department that was underpaid (moving towards my goal of "excellent pay"), and employee productivity increases to pay for the additional pay increases.

So, incentives are great, but there are basic elements that need to be present. You must have effective measurement tools. The incentive has to be enough to motivate employees into changing their behavior. The incentive plan has to be reasonably achievable. Most employees can recognize if they have a reasonable chance of earning the incentive. Use incentives and get lots of input before you implement them.

# HR Has a Place, But Let's Be Reasonable.

Over my forty some years in business, I have seen what was the Personnel Department evolve into what has become Human Resources. Certainly, business has become much more difficult due to government regulations at all levels, and our litigious society. HR always has the threat of what bad things can happen if we don't give employees warning, after warning, after warning, and document every thought and conversation we had on any employee subject.

I'm just thinking it may have gotten out of hand. Yes, we may have to pay unemployment, but sometimes in my book its worth it just to be rid of an exceptionally difficult person. I happen to believe that most people don't change. Sure, I have seen life changing events where people do change, but I have seldom seen employees changing bad behaviors based on their most recent review. If an employee is unaware of their poor behavior, perhaps they have the wherewithal to make a change, if they want to, but things like conflict with others, or always needing to be right, or first, can be tough to change. These things are deeply rooted, and part of their basic personality or psyche. In that case, the sooner they are gone the better. Twenty-six write-ups and constant warnings, are a poor approach in my opinion. The damage done to other employees and the morale of other employees (how can management let them get away with that?) can cost a lot more than six months of unemployment, in terms of productivity.

And yes, I understand that risks can be greater than just unemployment. There is age discrimination, racial discrimination, religious discrimination, and all kinds of other risks out there. My point is, sometimes it is worth the risk.

I clearly remember a receptionist who was convinced that it was O.K. to miss work, as long as she had a reasonable excuse. The problem was, as receptionist, when she was gone, someone had to sit at her desk, which took that person away from their normal duties, and their work didn't get done. Other employees very much resented the receptionist's absence, because it affected them. After a couple of warnings, we dismissed this employee, explaining that while her absences were explained, there were just too many of them.

## The Grapevine Exists. Use It to Your Advantage.

We can deny the existence of a grapevine as a means of communication or we can acknowledge and use it. I prefer the latter. There is no question that employees talk or that they tell each other things "in confidence". If you have been in and around almost any organization, it isn't hard to find out who is tuned in to the grapevine, i.e. there is usually a person who has reliable information on what is going on almost anywhere in the company. Managers can use the grapevine when they want information disseminated very quickly and with a fair amount of accuracy. Maybe we want to get a reaction to some proposed action by management or perhaps to calm nerves when there is unrest.

In an earlier chapter, I discussed using the grapevine to talk about a "secret program" where employees could receive increased pay by eliminating a position within their department. The grapevine worked well because the program wouldn't work in all departments, and was most effective when someone quit.

I believe we are much more effective using the grapevine, than trying to eliminate it or to try and find out its sources and shut them down. You are trying to defeat human nature. Be aware of, and use the grapevine to your advantage.

## What We Know for Sure About Forecasts and Plans.

I am a great believer in plans and forecasts. I also define a plan as being from one to five years and a forecast as being from one to eleven months and a revision to the annual plan. I think they are great tools to measure progress from period to period and year to year. Unfortunately, I think we spend unproductive time on putting a plan together and then trying to explain why it was wrong. One technique I observed was to subtract the highs and lows for the year, inflate revenue by some percent that we dreamed up or copied from somewhere else and that became our plan. The fact is, there are highs and lows every year, and various other "unplanned" events. I recall one owner who would spend an inordinate amount of time putting plans together at various over-inflated revenue increases. The owner would then show his executive team how profitable the company could be if only the revenue increases were achieved. Obviously, the more revenue you achieve over the breakeven point, the more profitable the company becomes. The problem was, the company had never achieved the annual revenue growth that was projected, and there was no specific strategy to achieve the new growth. When I told the owner that, I wasn't very popular.

What we know for sure about a plan or a forecast is that it is probably going to be wrong. We just don't know which way or by how much. In theory, a plan should be more accurate than a comparison to last year, but depending on the business, the year to year comparison works just fine. An exception would be where we, perhaps, add a new product line or the business has dramatic swings and we can anticipate them. Plans and forecasts are like analyzing an economy. There are just so many variables that are nearly impossible to predict.

Finally, I really believe an annual plan, and even a three year plan, can be of value. The plan allows us a method of determining where we expect growth and where we expect products to mature and go away. Measuring against the plan is also an effective tool. It may instill in us the necessity to plan for the futures of our business and to, perhaps, invest more in research and development. I've never been a fan of five or ten year planning unless it is on a very general basis. We can't predict the weather tomorrow so who knows where we may be in ten years.

Set up an effective planning process, not to lengthy, that involves all levels of employees.

## Everybody Sells.

A while ago, I served on a Business Advisory Council for one of the local universities. The purpose of the Council was to help the university develop courses which would be valued by businesses. My feeling was that the university didn't spend enough time on teaching students to develop sales skills. It pretty much fell on deaf ears. At the same time, I was CEO for a local chemical company. The "sales" portion of the Sales and Marketing course really didn't exist. In reality, it was a Marketing course. I recited to the Council that I had two people in Human Resources, five people in Accounting, three people in Data Processing (this was before Information Systems), ten people in the warehouse, and TWO HUNDRED AND FIFTY Sales people. "Does that tell you something", I asked the Council? Many of our sales people were college graduates, so I would bet that most of those college graduates were not working in their "Majors".

I believe everybody sells on a daily basis, even if they don't have the word "sales" in their position title. We are constantly trying to convince our co-workers, supervisors, vendors, AND customers of something. Maybe we want to convince our boss to take some action. Maybe we are trying to convince someone in the next department to get some information that we need. Maybe we are trying to convince a vendor to ship something earlier. Sales techniques can be used by all of us in our business lives on a near constant basis. If we treated each other like customers, maybe our business relationships would improve. Perhaps there could be a little less yelling in the world?

I believe that employee training in sales techniques is worth the investment in time and money. Do it!

*"Nothing Happens Until Somebody Sells Something"*.

# Don't Transfer Employee Problems. Deal with Them Once.

How often have we seen an employee who causes problems in any department of the company and everybody knows it? Department managers often find it easier to transfer an employee to another department, in hopes that the employee will be "happier" somewhere else. I always felt that was pretty much of an excuse to avoid documenting and dismissing the employee. Don't let that happen. Be wary of transfers that aren't genuine promotions or where we are transferring a mediocre employee.

The biggest problem, often, is the employee who has been tolerated for many years. My advice is to "pull the trigger" and deal with the consequences. Some employees are more expensive to dismiss than others. At the same time, some employees are worth spending more for relief of the problem!

I fully realize that some people are quite happy in jobs that others may abhor. Try taking an outside sales person and putting them behind a desk. I always tried to be sure people were "on the right bus and in the right seat". Typically, the happier an employee is, the more productive he or she is. When an employee seems to be having trouble with productivity, it is helpful to get to the bottom of the issue. Don't transfer it away.

# I Have a Job for the Most Critical Person I Know.

In every company that I have worked for, there always seems to be that individual that finds fault with nearly everything. We may describe them as bitter, or angry or "not a team player". Well, I think there is a place in this world for those types of individuals. I'd like one of them to serve on my Board of Directors. Why is that? The person who finds fault with everything may just come up with some very legitimate points in almost any discussion of issues facing the company. I'd like to hear those criticisms before we proceed with a project.

There is another requirement for open and honest and critical discussions, and that is the reactions of senior managers. If they get angry, or defensive when criticisms are made, that can shut down employee comments pretty quickly. That is not conducive to productive and accurate conclusions. The CEO has to set the example with openness to any criticisms. At the same, time employee criticisms must be respectful, accurate, well thought out, and on point.

I am reminded of a business owner that I knew who was a tyrant to everyone and everybody. Disagree with him in a meeting, and you were soundly reprimanded. The message to everyone in the room was don't speak up or you will end up being shamed. That shuts down discussion pretty quickly and makes for shorter meetings. As I came in for the turnaround, it occurred to me that we had a whole lot of "yes" people, who wouldn't even speak up. That's what happens over time. The only employees who can survive are the ones who simply don't say anything. I find that tragic. Encourage your employees to speak up.

## Don't Try to Make Money on the Backs of Your Employees.
## Don't Cut Wages and Salaries.

When we are in business, there are really only two ways to increase profitability. Increase revenue or reduce expenses. We can make the situation a lot more complicated, but basically that's it. Increasing revenue? I think that is harder than reducing expenses. What does it mean? Sell more. Selling is one of the hardest, most stressful jobs out there. How many times have we seen a business for sale when the existing owner tells us, "it's a great business, it just needs more sales", Really? That's all?

I think that might be the reason that many business owners find it easier to try to reduce expenses. The expenses are right in front of us. We write checks for them all the time. Expenses are right under our noses. Because payroll is generally a big part of our expenses, it's easy to look in the most convenient places. My experience tells me, don't do it. Employees will sometimes find a way to make up for what they believe they lost. That could be taking office supplies, taking inventory, or in a retail or restaurant setting, finding a way to tamper with that flawless point of sale system. I should also mention productivity. We want our employees to be as productive as possible, and that has a lot to do with employee attitudes.

I've seen situations in a bar setting where the employee serves four drinks, let's say for $20, but rings up two for $10 and enters the remaining $10 as a tip. It happens. I am aware of one bar owner who actually pays a person (who everyone thinks is a regular) to simply watch the employees ringing up drinks.

As business owners, we should treat our employees with honesty, integrity, and respect, and we should expect the same in return. Let's not complicate the employer/employee equation by taking advantage of our employees because it's easier. If things are really tough, it is better to lay off an additional person than to inflict more pain on existing employees, through pay cuts. An employee gets their nose rubbed in a pay cut every time they get paid. It's not easy to forget. Also, keep in mind that the employees that leave us for other jobs are usually some of our best employees.

One example of making money on the backs of employees is a vacation pay computation that I came across. Vacation pay is generally earned in the prior year for the current year. I've seen it earned each month or week in the prior year or all of it earned on, say, December 31. The difference in methods sometimes relates to quitting in a given year and whether you should be paid for all or a portion of next years vacation. In the original situation, I mentioned employees had a hard time understanding when vacation was earned in the prior year or the current year. The vacation seemed to be earned in the prior year except when an employee requested fewer hours in the current year, the vacation for the current year was also reduced ("but I thought I earned that last year"). In addition, Saturday hours were not used in the vacation computation—even though this was a retail establishment that was open every Saturday. So if an employee worked Tuesday through Saturday they were credited with 32 hours of vacation credit for the week. If they worked Monday through Friday they received 40 hours of vacation credit. That could be another reason for not wanting to work Saturdays! Between these two situations, this of course caused a lot of anger among employees. I saw no point in doing what this employer did over a few hours of vacation. Clearly, when employees don't understand what you are doing, it is likely they will think you are trying to take advantage of them.

# Annual Reviews are Unnecessary if We Talk Every Day.

I often wonder where the idea of an annual or semi-annual review originated. The idea was certainly around when I began my work career in 1969-70. I clearly remember the drudgery of filling out review forms for the people I supervised. And if you didn't complete the form, the employee didn't get their pay increase. It seemed strange - the supervisor didn't do something and the employee got penalized. What justice!

What I found most effective was to communicate all the time. If I am upset with something an employee did or didn't do, why wait for a review? I want to talk about it now. Why stew about it for months, when the whole issue might have been a big misunderstanding.

A part of this is providing feedback (criticism?) to an employee and then giving them a raise. Then they stew about what you had to say for a few days or a few weeks, write their response, which then upsets the supervisor. Honestly, let's make course corrections along the way, instead of saving them up. Additionally, it always seemed to me that a review was a whole bunch of criticism with very few positives to be found. Maybe that was just me, but I never recall looking forward to a review. I wonder how many people do.

Here is the bottom line. Ultimately, the purpose of a review is to determine whether we get to keep our job for a while longer. I always knew who I wanted to be part of my team. I didn't need to do a calculation.

## The Moral CEO. Be Honest and Forthright with All.

Employees watch you and your body language. Be careful of how you walk, talk, and conduct yourself. Act happy and they see you as happy. Look worried and they become worried.

Insist that your managers act professionally. Employees tend to act like their bosses. If the boss flies off the handle—it's OK for them to fly off the handle. If their boss makes off color remarks—it's OK for them to do that. That leads to difficulty on many levels. Tell the truth, answer questions directly, and don't sound like a politician. You are not running for office. And remember, your employees are watching.

Manage objectively (honestly). If employees understand where the business is going, decisions will be perceived as non-political. We are investing in this product and phasing out that product. It isn't because the boss "likes" those employees in one department more than others.

My background includes a heavy dose of "turnaround" situations, in the fields of construction machinery, steel castings, chemicals and non-profits. Those are very different industries, but in many ways the same. Honesty is the best policy. In a turnaround, after we have a business worth saving and after the mandatory staff layoffs, I would announce that the staff reductions were over (cut once, cut deep), and that the remaining employees were the survivors. We were now going to work together to re-build this business. I had done it before and I will do it again. I discussed the importance of honesty in all of our dealings-with each other, with me, with vendors and with customers.

I pledge that I will always answer a question to the best of my ability and in an honest manner. I expect the same from all employees. That is a policy that is a key to our working for mutual success. I followed the same rule in working with vendors. I never lied about when someone would get paid. If I hoped to make a payment on Friday, I said exactly that, and I did my very best to keep my word. If I was unable to keep my word, I called the vendor and told them so, and why.

I would share my vision for the company, particularly as it related to employees, and I meant every word. I wanted our company to be an exceptional place to work. I wanted exceptional employees who would be paid in an exceptional way and enjoy exceptional benefits. It may take a while to get there and it wouldn't be easy, but we could and would do it. I also explained that we couldn't just increase wages and benefits over night, but as sales increased and productivity increased, wages and benefits would be a priority.

*Always be honest. Then you don't have to remember what you said.*

# So, Who Owes Who, What?

Organized Labor has long felt that companies are built by the employees, and therefore the company owes the employees everything. By the same token, the owners of companies often feel the company belongs to them. They built it with their capital; they put in long hours, and took great risks. There is truth on both sides. In my view, what works most effectively is an owner that recognizes the part that employees played in the success of the company. I've seen owners who love their employees like their own family and when business conditions deteriorate, the owners are more likely to endure significant financial pain before they impose any hardship on their employees.

In turnaround situations, it has been my observation that owners tend to be eternal optimists, believing things will get better soon, but with no credible plan to make that happen. That optimism can lead to trouble with bank loans and trouble with the banker. It does not take the turnaround consultant long to determine if the business owner is "ready" to accept the advice of the consultant. "We can't do that!" doesn't fly, and is the indicator that the owner is not "ready" and the consultant is wasting his breath. When the owner is saying "I simply do not know what to do, I don't have any more money, and I am willing to do whatever it takes to save my company", that tells me the owner is ready to listen. The next hardest step is making the hard choices as to who stays with the company and who gets laid off. I have had owners tell me "you have to do the layoffs. I just can't do it". Those owners cared about their employees. I always looked at it as; some employees had to go so that others could keep their jobs.

As for "who owes who", I think both owners and employees owe each other. Each has to appreciate the contributions of the other. Neither could make it without the other. I said earlier that I always wanted to have a company that was a good place to work, that had excellent products, excellent workers, with excellent pay and benefits. I still feel the same way. Sincerely care about your employees.

## On Raising Prices.

I wrote earlier about the need for expense control and the need to increase revenue. For a while, I worked for a very old but struggling steel foundry. I should mention that the company was getting a lot of small casting work and I wondered why this small foundry in Wisconsin was taking work away from a lot of foundries that were much bigger and much more efficient than we were. Also, the owner kept telling the sales department that we needed to sell bigger castings. I looked at the way we did pricing. Pricing was done on manufacturing cost plus mark up and manufacturing burden (mostly finishing) was assigned on a per pound of casting basis. Simply, that formula says the cost of finishing one 100 pound casting was the same as finishing 100 one pound castings. Obviously, that is not true. Finishing 100 small castings takes a lot longer than finishing one 100 pound casting. For illustration purposes, I used examples that applied finishing cost on a per casting basis. That made small castings a lot more expensive to finish but represented a close approximation of actual cost. It became clear that the reason we were getting a lot of small work was because we were significantly under pricing our small work. I tried to get the owner to see what was happening, but he wouldn't hear of it. I was telling him that the only work he was getting was because he was under pricing the product. He wouldn't listen to me, and he owned the place, so I decided to leave, telling him that he would fill up capacity with small work and would still lose money. I was right, and he went bankrupt a few years later.

My next company was a chemical company. It was a medium sized company that had been, and should still be, very, very profitable. I found the lack of profitability was, in part, related to pricing. They hadn't adjusted selling prices in more than eight years! Imagine that. If costs, overall, increased on average a nominal 3% per year, over eight years you have lost 24 margin points. Your question is why didn't we raise prices? The answer was because the sales people didn't like it when prices were raised, because the product became harder to sell.

My advice is to carefully monitor pricing on a very regular basis. It is a critical part of your success.

# On Hiring.

I have found over the years that my managers had a tendency to try to hire themselves. It makes sense doesn't it? I'm so good at everything I should try and hire someone just like me. Often times that was dead wrong. I was aware of one company president who had one sales manager who he would instruct to rate his candidates one through ten or one through 20, with number one being the best and number 10 being the worst. Once the sales manager did that he would tell him to hire number 10 or number 20. The idea was that the sales manager made the worst choice as his number one. True story!

Hiring people has become a lot more difficult because of government regulations on discrimination, eager lawyers, and a legal system that seems to favor "victims". It was always my intention to follow every law to the letter. That was the way I conducted business every day. Another new twist since I began hiring many years ago was the issue of dishonesty on applications or resumes. Maybe that is the result of a much more competitive market and job candidates who have exceptional qualifications. Let's also assume we have a pool of good candidates who haven't lied on their submissions, applications and resumes. I liked to interview the top 10 candidates via telephone and then decide how many I would like to interview in person. Let's assume we don't have an expensive distance problem with the interviews. Based on the telephone interviews, I would decide how many candidates I want to meet in person. I should point out that I was never a fan of having Human Resources interview the candidates and then presenting me "the" candidate. I also am not a fan of group interviews where 5 or 6 peers "grill" the candidate for an hour or so. I clearly remember participating on a search committee to select a new dean for a university school of business. It was a nightmare. All of the direct reports were part of the search committee, plus the VP of Academic Affairs, the head of HR, and me, a representative of the Business Advisory Board for the university. It took forever, at least 6 months from beginning to end, and in my opinion we ended up with a lousy candidate who lasted less than a year. I think I could have concluded the hiring process in a few weeks by myself.

So here is my process. I review all incoming resumes. I have three preliminary divisions. Yes. No. And maybe. I then proceed with telephone interviews for the top five or ten candidates. Essentially, I like to review what is on the resume and be sure to tell the person the salary range. I see no point in wasting the candidates time or mine, if the money doesn't work. I can usually pick out the resumes that were professionally written, and I view those with skepticism. I am also a stickler for proper spelling and grammar. I feel if you really want a job, you will be very careful about spelling and grammar. It was not unusual for me to exclude a resume for errors.

Based on the telephone interviews, I ranked candidates and scheduled personal visits. I am willing to meet anytime: early in the morning, in the evening, or on Saturday. I am very aware of how difficult it can be to get away from a responsible position for a preliminary interview. There are lots of interview questions out there, and I have just two comments. I believe the questions should be pretty consistent between candidates and my favorite interview question is "Tell me about your parents". As far as I know, there is no law about asking that, and I never had a candidate object to answering that question. What I'm looking for is insight into work ethic. If mom and dad worked very hard, chances are the kids will behave in a similar manner. That is a big factor in my mind.

I also believe that if a resume is honest, I can pretty well tell if the candidate can do the job I have available, so the major factor that is left is whether we can work together. That's what I want to determine in my process. Based on the face to face interview, I usually rate my candidates, 1, 2, and 3. How closely they rate determines whether or not I schedule another interview, where I may involve other interested parties. If I have a very clear front runner, I begin working on that candidate right now. Hopefully, I can hire my first choice!

Finally, I liked to play a strong role in the hiring of anyone for my division. If I have a supervisor who is hiring someone, I want to carefully review ALL the resumes and have a good understanding of my supervisor's process.

## On Firing.

There are two clear aspects on this subject: firing someone and getting fired. I've been fired twice. Both firings were significantly political, but as they say, the closer you get to the top, the less job security you have. Judges aren't real sympathetic when you are the top person and you are out of your well-paying job. I should also say that each time I was fired, I was led to bigger and better things, and new areas of interest. After my first firing, I spent a lot of time thinking about what I really wanted, and discovered what I really enjoyed was helping people. I started a small business with my son selling promotional items and discovered it was easier to sell if I concentrated on "helping" rather than "selling". What is the difference? Selling means I have a number of products that I try to convince you to buy. Helping means I am trying to find a product that is going to benefit you and your business. Getting fired isn't so terrible, and I'm not the type to try and sue you for firing me. So, get over it, and move on to the new challenge.

On firing someone else, I think we waste too much time on trying to change someone who simply isn't a fit. Oh I know, we have to document, document, document, and warn, warn, warn, warn, so let's get that out of the way, and find someone who is a fit. I am reminded of my friend who worked in a union shop and served as a union steward, but quit because he tired of trying to get jobs back for employees who deserved to be fired.

I also found that when I came into a new position, some of my subordinates could handle the change and some couldn't. I have my own way of doing things, and after lying in the weeds for a few months, I am likely to make changes, for the benefit of the company, the employee, or me. I liked hiring my own people because I found them to be more open to change, and not hung up on "the way we always did it before". Those new people were also more likely to be loyal to me. I like loyal employees.

# Office Affairs.

As long as there are men and women working together there is the potential for office affairs. Personally I don't cheat on my taxes. I don't cheat my customers, and I don't cheat on my wife. There are temptations everywhere in our daily lives, and we need to be strong enough to walk away from the temptation. That was my rule and that was the rule I had for my senior managers. If you want to have an affair don't use my workplace, and I would need to consider whether you are the person I thought you are.

This day in age there is significant company liability for a manager or supervisor, having a fling with a subordinate and it doesn't work out. We have the potential for a sexual harassment lawsuit, with all kinds of claims and counterclaims. I never wanted any part of that kind of a lawsuit and I let my senior managers know where I stood on the issue.

I had a senior manager, married with two young children who decided to have an affair with his new assistant. He was a very talented sales guy with lots of great customer relationships. NOT firing him was probably one of the harder things I had to do. I guess I was impressed with his forthrightness about his relationship and we had a long discussion about the potential liability the company was exposed to. He ended up marrying his assistant. Perhaps she was the love of his life as he had explained, and they are still married today at least twenty years later.

And just to show you that the grapevine can invent things, I remember a business trip to Las Vegas, whereupon returning, I had heard rumors that one of the ladies from a sister company had spent the night in my room. UNTRUE, of course. The good news for me was that my wife was with me on that trip and she was the only person who spent the night with me.

In summary, I guess I can understand temptation, and the effects of a few too many drinks, but the temptations and whatever his or her name might be, is also everywhere. Why risk your job and significant amounts of money for a fling. It just doesn't seem worth the risk to me. And as it tells us in the "The Millionaire Next Door:"

*Millionaires tend to get married and stay married.*

## Business Focus.

I'm pretty certain you may have run across the engineer/ entrepreneur who started a company with a brilliant idea and business kind of took off from there. The problem sometimes is the next brilliant idea and the next brilliant idea after that. The business needs to have enough cash to finance the ideas. Each dollar that comes in goes to finance the next brilliant idea.

I'm a believer in business focus. We sit down and decide what is really important to achieve and when. Maybe we set two or three priorities. It is then important to stay on each goal until we get where we want to be. That is focus. Business focus. We can't do everything or maybe we don't have enough cash to do everything. I pretty much spent my business life with struggling businesses. Cash was always an issue, and perhaps a good amount of that issue was in my worrying mind.

I know of a wonderful entrepreneur who started 5 or 6 businesses and described all of them as profitable within a year or two. I wonder. He was always looking for investors, but I wouldn't invest a dime. I see his businesses headed for trouble and the biggest problem is a lack of focus. The owner was doing so many different things, he wasn't doing a quality job at anything. That is to say nothing of co-mingling the incoming cash, and as far as I could tell, a lack of financial statements. His controller had quit, and that can often be a bad sign. The financial person is usually the first person to see things going in the wrong direction, and then they leave.

My advice is to carefully plan what we want to accomplish, how, and how much it will cost. Then we go ahead and do it, until it is finished or business conditions call for a change in direction—which we also carefully plan.

## The Field Sales Force.

From your prior reading in this book you can probably gather that I am sympathetic to sales people. It's a tough job where you are basically only as good as your last sale. In some ways, if you sell out of the home office, or are in the home office on a frequent basis, the feelings of detachment can be a lot less. The loneliest folks in the company are the field sales people who are alone and usually work out of an office in their home, or their car. I was often amazed at how the feeling of detachment these employees felt were so easily dismissed by management. The field sales people need to feel like they are a part of the company in order to be most effective at their jobs. That calls for more than the weekly company newsletter. It calls for regular attention from their manager, who is not too busy to listen. It calls for regular face to face sales meetings where they can talk to other salespeople about the issues and problems they face everyday. National sales meetings are great for building enthusiasm and in my mind, worth every penny they cost. I was also a believer in support people from the home office traveling with the field sales people. It was great for building employee rapport because the two parties got a good idea on how each accomplished their duties.

I had a boss a long time ago who required each person on his staff to travel one week in the spring and one week in the fall with a different sales person. I thought it was great. The sales person was usually flattered, to introduce his customers to someone from the home office, and as the home office person, I enjoyed meeting real life customers and hearing their stories. Something for you to consider.

## Saving Good Employees, Maybe From Themselves.

On a number of occasions I have had a really good employee go sour on me. By that I mean this was an employee who always seemed happy, showed up on time and did really good work. Suddenly, that employee turned sullen and seemed angry at everything and everybody. I made genuine efforts to find out what the problem was, but the employee wouldn't share what was wrong. As far as I could tell, it wasn't a work life issue but probably a personal issue that was spilling over into the work place. It was necessary to let the employee know that their attitude wasn't going to fly for very long.

My method was to have a serious meeting with the employee, explain that there was a noticeable change in their attitude and I could only surmise that they were not happy at our workplace any longer. Without hesitating for a comment from the employee, I would continue that I wanted them to be happy and as a result I would give them time off to search for other employment. I couldn't pay them for the time off but they were welcome to take time for interviews, etc. If they were unable to find other employment in, say three months, we would just have to part company.

Generally, what I had to say, was met with shock and disbelief. I didn't invite any further conversation at the time. The idea was to provide some shock and then let it settle in, at least overnight. Setting a deadline of three months emphasized that the employee was close to being let go, but in view of their past excellent service, I was going to give them time to find another job.

This process worked very well for me. Generally I had the employee come back in a day or so, and tell me they wanted to keep their job. I would see their attitude change and in every case it did. Often the employee would then share what was bothering them and 99% of the time it was a serious personal issue. I never had this process backfire, or had an employee take me up on seeking other employment.

Sometimes it is just necessary for the employee to understand that their poor attitude isn't acceptable and that they can and will be fired if it continues.

# Free Markets.

I am a believer in free and open markets and that the best way to control businesses is by letting the markets work. If a businessman is not honest in his dealings, word will get around and customers will stop coming through the door, and businesses seem to fail without customers.

I am not a fan of government regulations. I believe they generally make business more complicated and more expensive to conduct. I also believe that business people have a responsibility to the community and environment in which they live and I freely admit that over the years business people have abused their employees and surroundings.

Where things seem to get out of hand are where there are multiple layers of government all trying to regulate business. Federal regulations, State regulations, County regulations, and City regulations, layer after layer.

A small business owner can have a difficult time just being aware of all the regulations that affect his business much less complying with the many layers of government.

# Don't Do Dumb Things.

Sounds really simple doesn't it? But sometimes it is really hard to remember. I think we let related issues cloud our judgment and we end up doing dumb things or what appears to be dumb things to other people. A number of other chapters in this book could be interpreted as cautions against doing dumb things. For instance, if we were to try to make money on the backs of our employees, that would turn out to be a dumb thing to do.

I recently attended a food sampling event at a local zoo. The food was terrific. It was a beautiful summer evening and there was a long line before the gates opened. The zoo had a very nice gift shop but unfortunately it was closed before the event. So you have a bunch of people standing around outside the gift shop who have time and probably money but the gift shop is closed!?!?! Doesn't make sense to me.

Another example was a winery I worked with, that had a rather small tasting room and one of the principals noticed people were leaving because there wasn't much room and they couldn't get close to the sample bar. People seemed to take a chair at the bar and stay there all afternoon. I asked if the winery charged for samples of the wine and the answer was "no". I asked if the winery across the street charged for samples and the answer was "yes".

No wonder people came into the winery and didn't leave. Free wine here, but not across the street.

Sometimes, I can't see the reasoning. Why would you do that? Is it a case of not thinking or some other reasoning that I don't understand. The other thing that surprises me is that employees don't take notice and bring up the issue.

Perhaps the employees may think that their thoughts don't matter. That would be too bad. Then again, maybe it goes back to my chapter on "Thinking is Hard Work," and that's why we don't see more of it."

# On Looking Good.

Dress codes for work seemed to become much more lax over my work career. I have worked in places with pretty strict dress codes and places where the dress code was pretty loose. I am sincere when I say I don't think a more lax dress code makes for less work being accomplished. I do believe however, that senior managers should look professional and well dressed even in casual clothes. I like jeans and I happen to believe that expensive jeans fit better than cheap ones. I do believe I have paid more for some of my jeans than I have for some of my suits! A pair of jeans that fits well, a crisp white or blue shirt can be comfortable and professional. I also prefer well shined shoes. I am amazed at the number of men I see in very nice suits with shoes that haven't seen polish in a long time. Ruins the effect for me. Finally I don't think anything looks better or makes me feel better than the dark blue suit, white shirt with cufflinks, a great tie, and spit shined shoes.

There is another aspect to looking successful, however. Let's use the example of a business consultant. Do you want to hire a consultant who looks successful, with a nice suit, gold rings, and bracelets and a nice watch? I do. I want a person who is obviously successful at what they do. That goes for the car as well. Cars spell success and a car that is falling apart doesn't show me success. It doesn't have to be a Mercedes, a nice Camry will do. The wife can drive the BMW. I am reminded of a good friend, a retired university professor who did a lot of presentations. He was always very nicely dressed in an expensive suit and tie that fit well. He wore well maintained shoes. He had a habit of really getting into his presentations by waving his arms around quite a bit. That would reveal his plastic "Iron Man" watch. I explained to him, that I thought it ruined the effect-either buy a new decent watch, or at least take off the "Iron Man". He bought a new watch.

I learned another lesson from a sales manager I knew. He wanted me (as President) to look well paid. He bought me a Rolex watch (through the company) and a company ring that resembled a Superbowl ring with lots of diamonds. The idea was to make our salespeople want what we were wearing. They could win the ring and the diamonds and the Rolex. It made sense to me and I was amazed at how many sales people wanted a ring like I wore. Look the part!

## Answering E-mails and Telephone Calls.

I always felt that if I didn't respond to an e-mail or telephone call that I was being rude. Let me qualify that. I didn't feel it necessary to respond to unsolicited e-mails or telephone cold calls. But if I had a concern from an employee or associate I feel it is necessary to respond even if a response wasn't requested. Maybe it was simply a "Thanks" so the person knew I received and read their message. If they asked me a question, I answered the question or referred it to someone who could answer the question. If I referred the question to someone else, I let the questioner know that they could expect a response from so and so, and if they didn't receive a response on a timely basis to please contact me again.

Why is it some folks don't respond to the e-mails and telephone calls they receive. Many reasons I suppose. I have certainly heard, "I am too busy" or "I receive so many e-mails, I can't respond to all of them". I think that is just plain arrogance. I know a lot of busy people from college professors to CEO's who habitually answer the inquiries they receive. I respect that and them for doing so.

It seems to me common courtesy has taken a beating over the years and that's just too bad. Maybe we can reverse the trend in part, by providing some common courtesy to our associates.

## Having A Job Is Like Having A Bank Account.
## (Jerry)

As a final chapter in this book, I have some advice for employees.

Having a job is much like having a bank account, a dear friend of mine used to say. If you make deposits you can make withdrawals. If you don't make any deposits you can't make any withdrawals.

What does that mean to me? I believe employees need to exceed their manager's expectations. Be dependable, maybe early for the work day, willing to stay late when it is required and supportive of their managers. Maybe it means making helpful suggestions to make the department and the company a better place to work. Sometimes maybe we call it being a team player or a company person.

When we have that team player we may be able to ask for a withdrawal here and there. Maybe it means some time off for a doctor's appointment or to attend a child's soccer game. I just believe a manager has a lot easier time saying yes to an employee who is always willing to go the extra distance. That of course is opposed to the employee who arrives for work 1 minute ahead of time or a few minutes late, takes extra time on breaks and lunch hours, is often sick or has any number catastrophes which consistently keeps them from their work.

I encourage employees to be aware of the deposits and withdrawals they are making. In my mind the deposits must always exceed the withdrawals. Just like a bank account.

# A Tribute To My Friend Jerry.

Now let me say a word about my dear friend who originated two prior chapters. Jerry was a vice president of manufacturing at the steel foundry where I was vice president of finance. I left the foundry because I felt the company was going down the wrong path to profitability. Jerry stayed. A number of his brothers, cousins and other relatives worked for the foundry also. Jerry loved people and all of his employees. He could be really tough and really caring. He desperately loved his wife, son, and a sister that he had raised when his parents passed away. I learned a lot from him about how to handle people under many different circumstances. He also taught me some valuable lessons in dealing with my kids, namely unconditional love and its real meaning.

As I said, I left the foundry for greener pastures. Jerry stayed as the company went downhill. I was told that another senior manager blamed Jerry for a lot of the difficulties the company was having. That was completely untrue. The company was having trouble because of their pricing formula. But Jerry was apparently convinced that at least some of the problems were of his doing. That meant that many of Jerry's friends and relatives could lose their jobs if the company closed.

From the circumstances, it appeared Jerry could no longer go on living. I really miss the guy and I wish, maybe I could have done or said something that might have helped him in his difficult time.

So often it has been said that we should not judge our fellow human beings, because we don't know what their journey is really like. How true that is. Sometimes we can have a great impact by saying the wrong thing at the wrong time, or the right thing at the right time.

www.ingramcontent.com/pod-product-compliance
Lightning Source LLC
Chambersburg PA
CBHW021906170526
45157CB00005B/1989